Centre Pompidou

Philippe Bidaine

© 2000, Éditions Scala - Passage Lhomme - 26 rue de Charonne - 75011 Paris / Tous droits réservés   Scala   Centre Pompidou

A futuristic ship moored in the heart of Paris, the Pompidou Centre was bound to respect the history of the area it now occupies. Lying between the former Halles (market area) and the aristocratic Marais, the Beau-Bourg district (an ironic nickname because it was so poor and disreputable compared with the wealthy neighbouring parish of Saint-Merri) is delimited by two main roads: to the west by the Rue Saint-Martin

A sense of destiny

(the saint is said to have taken this route after
kissing and healing a leper) and, to the east, by
the Rue du Temple, which led to the precinct and
fortified keep of the Knights Templar. The
churches of Saint-Merri, Saint-Nicolas-des-
Champs and Saint-Martin-des-Champs (now the
Musée des Arts et Métiers) overshadowed a
labyrinth of streets ideal for ambushes, secret
meetings, riots and revolution.

∧ The Beaubourg and
Saint-Merri districts in
1615. Detail from map
by Mattäus Merian.

< Bird's-eye view of
the district from the
Pompidou Centre with
Notre-Dame at the back.

Artisans, intellectuals and artists

Many artisans and craftsmen set up shop in the Beaubourg district : butchers, curriers, cutlers, exchange agents, glaziers, needle-makers, pastry-cooks, saddlers and street vendors, as well as usurers and moneychangers (John Law established his banking business in the Rue Quincampoix). It was also a place of varied entertainment, featuring theatres, vividly named taverns (the Golden Eagle, the Cow with its Tail up, the Fishing Fox, etc.), hot-spots, bawdy houses and prostitutes.

There are many legends associated with it. For instance, the public scrivener Nicolas Flamel, after whom one of the streets is named, had accumulated an immense fortune and was believed to have discovered the philosophers' stone which changed lead into gold. And there was intense political activity, ranging from riots by the turbulent butchers' guild to the "queen's necklace" incident – a fraud in which Marie-Antoinette herself was implicated and which contributed to the fall of the monarchy.

Beginning in the 16th century, the district acquired an artistic and literary reputation. The Hôtel Jabach, a splendid town house built for the German financier Everhard Jabach by the architect Bullet in 1659, became a centre of cultural activity where the owner displayed his magnificent collection of works of art, and received and supported contemporary artists. After Jabach's death, the building was converted into an opera house and theatre. It was still standing in the early years of the 20th century on Place Saint-Merri, where it is now the location of IRCAM.

The Épée de Bois (Wooden Sword) tavern, in the Rue Quincampoix, was the venue for meetings of the dancing masters' and violin teachers' guild, which later gave birth to the Royal Academy of Dance and Music. At the Écharpe Royale (Royal Scarf tavern), Valentin Conrart and his friends Chapelain and Gombault presided over learned gatherings at which literature, recent publications and the purity of the French language were discussed. Fearing that this gathering might become a focus of opposition, Richelieu decided to make it an instrument of government policy by granting the writers pensions and establishing the Académie Française.

< The Rue Quincampoix in 1720, engraving by Humblot.

< The Rue Quincampoix in the 18th century, engraving by Régnier.

< The Rue Brisemiche in 1904, water-colour by Bellettre.

Inauguration du Boulevard de Sébastopol, le 5 avril 1858.

∧ **The Halles and the Rue de la Tonnellerie in the 19th century, by Canella.**

∧ **The opening of the Boulevard de Sébastopol, 5 April 1858.**

> **The church of Saint-Merri, engraving by Arnoult.**

The theatre was also a vital element in the life of the district, with real tennis courts first used to house drama productions. A troupe led by the actor Mondory then began staging plays by Scudéry, Quinault and Corneille at the Hôtel d'Argent (in the Rue de la Verrerie), prefiguring the Comédie-Française. Madame de Staël held her famous salon at the Hôtel d'Hallwyll, where she received eminent philosophers and writers.

Beaubourg is also associated with authors and poets. Boccaccio was born in the Rue des Lombards, as were, much later, Gérard de Nerval and Robert Desnos. The district has provided the setting for several novels : Victor Hugo drew on it for parts of *The Hunchback of Notre Dame* and *Les Misérables*; Restif de la Bretonne used it for the 183rd of his *Parisian Nights*; and Honoré de Balzac made it the home of César Birotteau. It was there that Gérard de Nerval met Aurélia; Robert Desnos and Guillaume Apollinaire celebrated it in their poems; and André Breton apostrophised it in *L'Amour fou* and *Arcane XVII*.

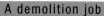

∧ The Beaubourg district after the war.

> Before the building of the Pompidou Centre, the Beaubourg site was a car park.

In the time of Napoleon III, Baron Haussmann, prefect of Paris, laid out the city's great boulevards, resulting in the demolition of many older districts. Beaubourg, now cut off by two major traffic arteries (the Rue de Rivoli and the Boulevard de Sébastopol), gradually declined. Classed as a slum, much of the district was demolished between 1933 and 1937, leaving the Beaubourg and La Reynie areas as vacant sites. Until 1969, the Beaubourg plateau was occupied by a car park and a workshop recycling boxes and packing cases in relation with the Halles activities. In 1968, the authorities decided to redevelop the site. Restoration projects were carried out in the Rue Saint-Merry, the Rue Michel-le-Comte and the Rue Quincampoix, then in 1969 Georges Pompidou decided to build a cultural centre on the plateau itself. The relocation of the Halles to Rungis provided an ideal opportunity to redevelop a huge area in the heart of Paris, on either side of the Boulevard de Sébastopol, devoted to culture and leisure.

A bold concept

"It is my passionate desire that Paris have a cultural centre [...] which is both a museum and a creative centre where the plastic arts can flourish alongside music, the cinema, books, audiovisual research, etc. The museum can only be devoted to modern art, as we already have the Louvre. The creative activities would of course be modern and in constant development. The library would attract thousands of readers who would therefore be brought into contact with the arts".

∧ Georges Pompidou
  by Vasarely, 1976.

< A new construction system :
  "the gerberette".

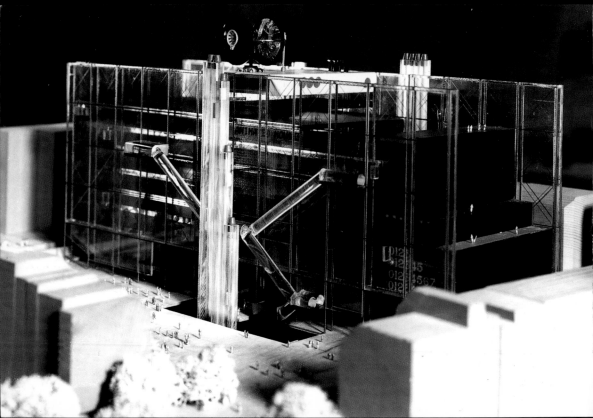

This was how, in 1969, Georges Pompidou, then President of the Republic, stated his intention for the site. A study group was set up to refine the concept and prepare for an international architectural competition. So exciting was the idea that 681 projects were received from all over the world. The specification had been clearly defined : a complex of integrated cultural facilities devoted to contemporary expressions of all artistic and cultural disciplines. On 15 July 1971, an international jury chaired by engineer Jean Prouvé and including many important figures from the world of architecture and the arts selected the project entered by two young architects, Renzo Piano and Richard Rogers, assisted by the design office of the Ove Arup Partnership. The jury's decision was based on a number of criteria : the extent to which the proposed building fulfilled the stated aims of the Centre, how it fitted into the district, the way the various activities were integrated in a single venue, flexibility of use, access and traffic flow, facilities for receiving and directing visitors.

^ The prize-winning architects, Renzo Piano and Richard Rogers, in the company of Robert Bordaz, first president of the Centre, and Pontus Hulten, director of the Musée National d'Art Moderne.

< The model of Renzo Piano and Richard Rogers' first project.

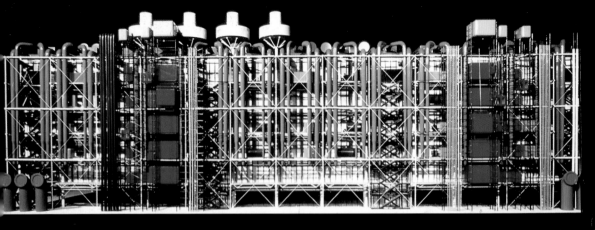

An original style of architecture

Renzo Piano and Richard Roger's project satisfied all these requirements, flexibility of use being ensured by the creation of vast uncluttered spaces and semi-independent facilities which could be modified according to need.

Far from imitating the surrounding buildings, the idea was to erect an unashamedly contemporary, hi-tech building, create a facade incorporating stairways and information about the activities available within, and turn half the site into an open space reflecting the life of the surrounding area. By pushing the main services (lifts, escalators, water, waste pipes, etc.) to the outside of the building, the architects succeeded

in freeing up the interior space and making the life of the place immediately visible. The structure consists of five vast tray-like floors, each 7,500 m² in area, without any intermediate walls or supports.

This transparent construction, open to the city, simultaneously utopian and realistic, combining past and present, forms a natural link between daily life and on-going creativity. From the top floor, 42 metres above the ground, Paris is revealed as a museum-city, which is why the Centre had to combine both past and present. The marriage of Gothic and hi-tech is a vivid illustration of the continuity of human genius.

∧ Model of the building :
the east and west facades.

A building site in the heart of Paris

The construction work lasted five years (1972 to 1977), during which this highly unusual building site evolved in full view of the general public, who could follow developments and learn about the technological exploits involved by taking one of the guided tours organised by architecture students.

In February 1997, the Georges Pompidou National Arts and Cultural Centre was inaugurated by President Giscard d'Estaing and at last opened its doors to the public.

∧ The foundations being laid.

< An artist rendering of the Centre in construction : Gordon Matta-Clark, *Conical Intersect*, photograph, 1975.

A technical challenge

Piano and Rogers's building is unique, on account of its previously untried construction system and of its materials, which at the time were the last word in steel technology.

The metal structure consists of fourteen frames/trusses set at 12.8-metre intervals, each composed of a pair of pillars 50 metres apart. At each level of the building, the pillars support moulded steel members known as "gerberettes" (after their inventor, the German engineer Gerber). The giant uprights which bear the metal framework are hollow and filled with water, to give the building greater stability and protection against fire. The columns of water are kept in motion by a pump, which will keep the structure

∧ Pillars, gerberettes and tie-rods.

< The metal framework completed.

rigid for at least two hours in the event of a disaster – long enough to evacuate the building. The inner end of each gerberette houses the end of an interior beam 50 metres long and weighing 70 tons. On the outside, this weight is balanced by a steel tie rod, anchored in the same concrete block as supports the pillar.

By this means, the load-bearing structure is relegated to the outer edges. The interior space is completely uncluttered and the five floors of the building are like immense trays, free of all encumbrance. Attached to the outside of the east facade, where they form a kind of cladding, the service ducts are painted in four different colours : blue for ventilation shafts, green for water and waste pipes, yellow for electrical wiring, red for stairways and escalators. Inside the building, services can be run to all points

∧ **Visitors reach the upper floors by an escalator which climbs the front of the building like a transparent caterpillar.**

through false floors, while rooms and exhibition areas are delimited by moveable partitions (sound or visual barriers, walls for hanging works of art, etc.).

Though totally original in appearance and technique, this style of architecture also has something neo-Gothic about it : a concern for light and airiness, a sense of space, the reduction of load-bearing surfaces, large areas in which people can circulate and gather.

The concept had been embodied in a suitable building. All that remained was to make it a special venue for exhibitions, debates, concerts – the whole heritage of the 20th century. Everything was ready to welcome the general public and bear witness to the creative genius of the age.

Overleaf : blue, green, yellow, red, the Centre is like a city with its heart laid bare.

An integrated activity centre

The Pompidou Centre is a place where the different forms of creative activity are brought together to explain and illustrate one another. During the 20th century, there was a great deal of cross-fertilisation between the visual arts, music, choreography and drama. The role of the Centre is to bring out these interconnections and

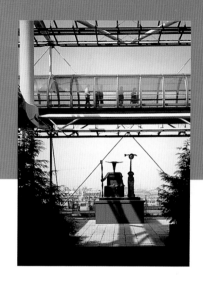

encourage today's creative artists to experiment in the same way. The Pompidou Centre is therefore organised on original lines : a public institution with a cultural purpose, operating under the aegis of the Ministry of Culture and run by its own president, it consists of two departments and two associated bodies.

∧ On the museum terrace,
Max Ernst's *Capricorne*.

< Neil Dawson's suspended
globe, a feature of the
1989 "Magiciens de la
Terre" exhibition.

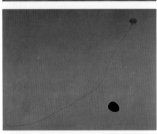

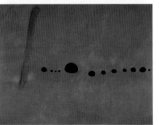

< In 1994, the museum
acquired *Bleu I*, bringing
together all three of
Joan Miró's works on
this theme.

> The Matisse room.

The first of the two departments is the Musée National d'Art Moderne, the only institution already in existence before the foundation of the Centre itself. The MNAM has continued the work of the Musée du Luxembourg (1818–1940), then devoted to living artists, the Musée du Jeu de Paume, devoted to non-French schools, the Musée National d'Art Moderne formerly housed in the Palais de Tokyo (1947–1976) and its adjunct, the Centre National d'Art Contemporain (established in 1986). The museum is the repository of collections of modern and contemporary art acquired by or bequeathed to the State, or handed over in lieu of taxation.

Housing one of the world's largest collections, with more than 40,000 works, the museum provides a remarkable insight into the many art forms practised during the 20th century. The conjunction of painting, sculpture, drawing, installations,

video art, films made by artists or architects and industrial design results in a fuller understanding of the creativity of the period. The museum is of course not large enough for the whole collection to be displayed at any one time, but in the interests of comprehensiveness works are exhibited in rotation, and are loaned for longer or shorter periods to regional museums as part of the museum's very active "extra-mural" policy.

The art of the first half of the 20th century is represented by about 900 works. Ranging from Fauvism to the American brand of Abstract Expressionism and the various movements of the 1950s (Klein, Soulages, Hantaï), they reveal the great wealth of the museum's collections : Cubist sculptures, works by some of the century's great masters (Matisse, Picasso, Braque, Duchamp, Kandinsky, Léger, Miró, Ernst, Giacometti, Dubuffet), and a diversity of groups and movements (Dada, Bauhaus, abstraction, informal art). Some of the highlights are the reconstruction of André Breton's studio, a room devoted to

∧ Francis Picabia, *Animal Trainer*, 1923, one of the most recent acquisitions.

< Giacometti's *Standing Woman II*, facing Francis Bacon's *Three Figures in a room* (detail).

Matisse's gouache cut-outs, and the terraces accommodating monumental sculptures.

The contemporary collections begin with a section devoted to Jean Tinguely and large groups of works illustrating artistic creation from the 1960s to the present day : Pop Art with Warhol, Oldenburg and Rauschenberg; New Realism with Arman and César; Poster, Op and Kinetic Art with Albers, Agam, Soto, Vasarely and Morellet; Arte Povera with Marz, Penone and Kounellis; and Conceptual Art with Dan Graham. Also represented are the new tendencies in figur-

ative and abstract painting, which impinge upon the Dubuffet, Kienholz, Bueys and Raynaud rooms. Plenty of space is given to the very latest developments, three rooms are devoted to the history of design and architecture, and one to the new media.

The museum maintains an archive with a wide range of material on 20th-century art, architecture and design, which can be consulted by researchers and students. It also helps organise displays of rare documents and carries out the documentary research required for exhibitions.

^ Views of two rooms devoted to the contemporary collections.

Brancusi's workshop

^ Brancusi in his workshop,
self-portrait, 1933–1934.
He was the subject of
a retrospective in 1995.

> Brancusi's workshop,
reconstructed in front
of the Centre in 1996.

During his lifetime, Brancusi "constructed" a workshop to display his sculptures at no. 11 Impasse Ronsin, in fact creating his own personal museum. He eventually bequeathed this workshop to the French State in 1956, on condition that it be recreated in a museum. It is now housed in a building designed by Renzo Piano, in front of the Pompidou Centre.

It was envisaged as a place of quiet contemplation, a place to wander among the artist's most significant works (*Bird in Space, Leda, Endless Column, Sleeping Muse*), as well as his plans, plinths, moulds and casts, work benches and tools.

Economie

Cultural development, BPI and IRCAM

The department of cultural development is responsible for the Centre's programme of debates and meetings, performing arts events (theatre and dance) and film shows. The exhibitions and talks it organises reflect the process of cultural, anthropological and sociological change in contemporary society. As well as its regular film cycles and dance events, it stages reviews and debates of a very high standard, at which famous writers, philosophers and scientists from France and abroad are invited to give their views on contemporary issues. A special place is reserved for the theatrical dimension of the visual arts as featured in concerts, dance events, performances, improvisations and "carte-blanche" sessions. The cinema is also well represented, with showings of fiction, ethnographic and art films, and video-dance festivals.

An associated institution which plays a large part in the life of the Centre is the Public Information Library (BPI), which can accommodate 2,000 readers, who enjoy free access to the library's material. Housing more than 500,000 books, visuals and films, it is one of the largest sources of self-service documentation available anywhere. Readers can consult books,

^ The Public Information Library (BPI) : books, magazines, films and CD-ROMs all within easy reach.

∧ The anechoic chamber at the IRCAM.

newspapers and magazines (400,000 items), view audio-visual material, use computers and multimedia workstations to surf the Net, listen to music and study in the language laboratory. The library, which is used by 10,000 people every day – of all ages and social backgrounds –, also contributes to the life of the Centre by organising exhibitions, debates and film festivals.

The Centre for Acoustical and Musical Research (IRCAM), the fourth body involved in the work of the Pompidou Centre, is located outside the building itself, partly under the Place Saint-Merri. The brainchild of Pierre Boulez, devoted to study and research in the musical field, this insti-tution welcomes musicians and researchers from all over the world, who can use its facilities to create new works and experiment with new tech-nology. These include studios, laboratories, anechoic rooms, a sound projection room, a mediatheque and all the latest technological developments. Many contemporary composers conduct their research at IRCAM and use it for public performances of their works. There is now a new section devoted to sound design (environ-ment and the urban setting), and a choreographic section is being developed. The Institute also has a university teaching function and attracts students doing a master's degree in musicology.

< The IRCAM building,
  by Renzo Piano, seen
  from the Centre.

A place of discovery

By creating a vast esplanade in front of the building, the architects wanted to remove any barrier between the Centre and the surrounding city. The Piazza is a magnet for open-air performers : fire-eaters, jugglers, musicians, caricaturists and story-tellers entertain the passers-by and plunge visitors to the Centre into an atmosphere of playful activity.

As a result of the pedestrianisation of many streets and squares, the creation of the Horloge district to the north, the new Halles district to the west and the restoration of the Marais district to the east, the Centre has become part of a large urban complex where people are encouraged to discover the city by foot.

∧ The Centre, right in the heart of the city.

< Live performances take place in the square and in the pedestrianised streets nearby.

> **Niki de Saint-Phalle and
Jean Tinguely's fountain**
in the Place Stravinski,
1983.

^ The forum, on the ground
floor, is a place of varied
encounters.

The Pompidou Centre was an immense success from the very outset. During the first weeks, each day more than 35,000 people flocked to see this new building. They may have been attracted partly by its idiosyncratic architecture, but there was also a great deal of interest in its prestigious exhibition programme.

The Pompidou Centre has since attracted over seven million visitors a year, welcoming, informing and entertaining devotees and discoverers of modern and contemporary art and culture, as well as all those who use the Library. The district is again full of life, having rediscovered its cultural vocation. The Centre has become one of the world's most popular cultural attractions, and one of France's most visited monuments.

∧ The wife of the sculptor
Jacques Lipchitz at the Centre
in 1978.

∧ Visitors to the Gerhard Richter
exhibition in 1978.

Major events

In its first year, the Centre staged a series of events the diversity of which demonstrated an intention to regale the public with culture in all its forms : a retrospective of the literary and artistic relationship between Paris and New York; a review of the work of the father of modern art, Marcel Duchamp; surveys of work in progress with Tinguely, Spoerri and Kienholz; drama with Eugène Ionesco and Calaferte; and encounters with Francis Ponge, André Frénaud, Nathalie Sarraute, Octavio Paz and William S. Burroughs.

In the years since the foundation of the Centre, there has been no decline in the ambition of the organisers, nor in the loyalty of the public. For twenty years, the Centre has put on many seminal

< The "Cartes et figures de la Terre" exhibition in 1980: displayed in the forum are globes built by the Venetian monk Coronelli.

< The logo of the "Paris-Berlin" exhibition, 1978, was designed by the graphic artist Roman Cieslewicz.

> The Tatlin Tower, a wooden
model for a monument to the
3rd Internationale (1920),
reconstructed for the "Paris-
Moscow" exhibition in 1979.

After "Paris-New York",
"Paris-Berlin" and
"Paris-Moscow", another
"Paris-Berlin" exhibition
in 1981.

events. Exhibitions — whether solo (Matisse, Brancusi, Delaunay, Le Corbusier, Pollock, Tanguy, Klein, Chirico, Balthus, Bonnard, Chagall, Kandinsky, Matta, Klee, Matisse, Picasso, Dali, Hockney, Breton, Eluard), collective or thematic (Paris-Berlin, Paris-Moscow, Vienna, Paris-Paris, forms of realism, maps and representations of the earth, contemplating history, masculine/feminine, the city, the art of the engineer), or temporary — have tended to draw on a whole complex of visual, literary, theatrical, philosophical and even musical components in developing their theme.

< A major acquisition : *Plight*
  by Joseph Beuys, 1985.

< Joseph Beuys at the Centre
  in 1984.

∧ Andy Warhol, *Campbell's
   Soup Can*, 1962.

∧ Andy Warhol in October
   1977, when he was
   the subject of
   a retrospective.

> *Ten Lizes* by Warhol,
   1963.

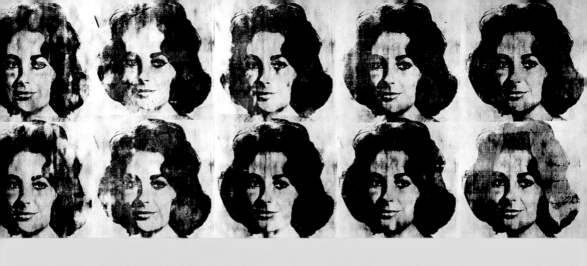

"25 May 1977... Pontus Hulten... arrived and took us around... We saw... Jean Tinguely's large sculpture in the forum... then the Kienholz exhibition, then the Paris-New York exhibition... as well as the permanent collection. It took two hours and Bob was on the point of fainting; but I was overflowing with energy and had only one desire : to rush home and paint and stop doing salon portraits."

Andy Warhol

The year 2000: a major refurbishment

After twenty years of constant and heavy use, it was time for the Centre to undergo renovation and be brought up to current health and safety standards, but without changing the way in which it was run and administered. Large sums were allocated by the State to implement the necessary improvements, and to provide the institution with more space to house and display its growing collections and performing arts activities.

As a result, the administrative services were moved out to nearby premises, and the interior areas of the building were redesigned and redistributed, thus gaining almost 8,000 m² of additional space (4,500 m² of which for the museum). New facilities were created for the performing arts. Special care was lavished on the reception area and services (bookshop, boutique, bar, restaurant), making them larger, more user-friendly and visually attractive.

∧ The works being moved.

< The top of the escalator, a walkway suspended between heaven and earth.

Double page overleaf : work in progress on the forum and basement level one.

Renzo Piano was commissioned to renovate the reception and performing arts areas, the exhibition area on the first floor, the terraces, and the service and access facilities. The young architectural team of Jakob and MacFarlane won the competition to redesign the top-floor restaurant, while the areas devoted to the permanent collections and library were given a new look by architect Jean-François Bodin.

A very full programme is planned for the year 2000 and subsequent years. There will be multidisciplinary exhibitions focusing on society (Le

temps vite/Time Flies, Les Arts ménagers/Home Economics, Regards d'un siècle/Looking Back on a Century), contemporary creativity (Jour de fête/Festival, Elysian Fields, Sons et lumières, L'Age du divertissement/The Entertainment Age, Pierre Huygue), solo exhibitions featuring great artists (Brassaï, Picasso as sculptor, Jean Dubuffet, Renzo Piano, Raymond Hains, Daniel Buren) movements (the Pop years, the Surrealist revolution), and the graphic arts (Giacometti, Rosemarie Trockel, Duchamp, Boltanski), as well as regular showings of new acquisitions, events

^ **Two views of renovated exhibition rooms.**

> *Giant Ice Bag*,
1969–1970, by Claes
Oldenburg, installed
in the year 2000.

for younger visitors, and displays of contemporary architecture, design, fashion and graphics.

The programme for the years ahead has a dual purpose : to continue the analysis of 20th-century art through the work of its most influential artists and, taking the analysis a stage further, to study the social developments of the period; and to examine and anticipate contemporary creativity by giving a free hand to artists, musicians and groups, presenting new research (e.g. in the fields of architecture and design), organising debates, and doing everything possible to develop and illustrate creative thinking.

A new Centre for a new generation. As the 21st century dawns, it is essential that the Pompidou Centre affirms yet again its commitment to the modern world.

Information

A FEW FIGURES

Height : 42 m
Length :166 m
Width : 60 m
Area of each floor : 7,500 m^2
Glass surfaces : 11,000 m^2
Non-glass surfaces : 7,000 m^2
Weight : 15,000 t

THE REFURBISHMENT (1997-1999)

A total area of 70,000 m^2 was refurbished in just 27 months.
In the Forum area, two bays were re-engineered to create two mezzanine floors, and new stairways and lifts were installed to link the three levels. The library was given a new entrance and the interior reorganised to improve traffic flow.
The electrical circuits, air-conditioning, fire-prevention systems and heating installations were all renewed.

ENTRY ARRANGEMENTS

The Georges Pompidou National Arts and Cultural Centre is open every day, except Tuesday, from 11 a.m. to 9 p.m. However, there is some variation in the schedules of the different activities, to take account of visiting habits and cultural practices :
The Musée National d'Art Moderne and exhibitions open at 11 a.m. (9.30 a.m. for group visits) and close at 9 p.m. every day.
The Public Information Library is open from 12 noon to 10 p.m. (11 a.m. to 10 p.m. on Saturdays and Sundays).

Live performances, film projections, meetings, lectures and concerts may go on beyond 10 p.m. depending on the scheduling of individual events. Admittance to the Public Information Library is free of charge. Access to the upper floors (by the escalator or lifts) is gained by payment of the museum entry charge (30F, reduced charge 20F) or the entry charge for temporary exhibitions (40F or 50F depending on the scale of the exhibition).

Photographic acknowledgements

Illustrations come from Pompidou Centre
documentation (Faujour, Meguerditchian, Migeat,
Prévost, Rich), with the following exceptions :
©ADAGP Paris, 2000
AKG Paris : p. 52
Archipress / Luc Boegly : p. 55
Bernard Vincent : p. 18
C.D.A. / Edimedia : p. 2, 40
Laurent Rousseau : p. 17
Photothèque des musées de la Ville de Paris :
p. 3 (Andréani), 4 (Degraces, Joffre), 6 (Ladet),
7 (Toumazet)
Rapho, Paris : p. 36 (Marc Tulane), 45 (De Sazo),
63 (C. Santos)

Editing : Chloé Demey
Translation : Simon Knight
Graphic design : delepière**damour**
Photoengraving : Offset photogravure, Maisons-Alfort
Printing : Editoriale, Italie
Copyright registered : february 2000